Grandma's Budgie

By Jack Gabolinscy
Illustrated by Astrid Matijasevich

Grandma's BUDGIE

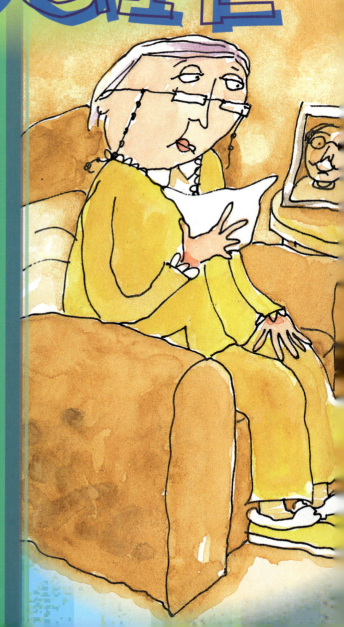

Everybody was sad when Grandpa died. Grandma cried, Mum and Dad cried, and I cried, too. I held Grandma's hand so she didn't feel so bad.

Next day Mum and I visited Grandma. When she saw us, she started crying again. I knew she was lonely because Grandpa was gone.

I said, "You can have one of my budgies, Grandma. Then you won't be lonely."

"Shhh!" said Mum. "Leave Grandma alone."

Grandma smiled through her tears. "What a good idea," she said. "I'd like that."

I gave Grandma a pretty blue and white budgie. He was the cheekiest and noisiest of them all. She put his cage on the table beside her rocking chair.

"I'll call him Peter, after Grandpa," she said.

Grandma and Peter were good friends. Grandma laughed when he hung upside down on his swing and rang his bell. She laughed when he looked in his mirror and squawked loudly as if he were talking to a friend.

Grandma loved watching Peter fly around in circles when she let him out to stretch his wings. She laughed when he flew down and landed on her head. She even laughed when it was time for him to go back into his cage and he wouldn't.

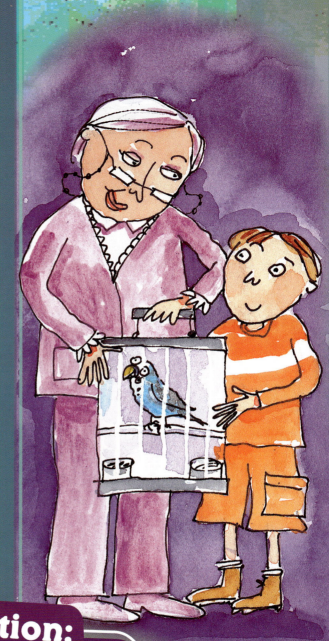

Question:

Why do you think the narrator gave Grandma the cheekiest, noisiest budgie?

Grandma said, "I'll teach Peter to talk."

"Budgies can't talk," I told her.

But I was wrong. Before long, Peter was talking, like a non-stop wind-up CD deck on fast speed.

"Peter's a pretty boy! Peter's a pretty boy! Peter's a pretty boy!"

Soon he could say lots of words. Whenever there was a quiet moment, his cheeky voice sang out through Grandma's lounge.

Good morning, Grandma!
Hello! Hello! Hello!
Bedtime, Peter!
Giz a bickie!
Wake up, Grandma!

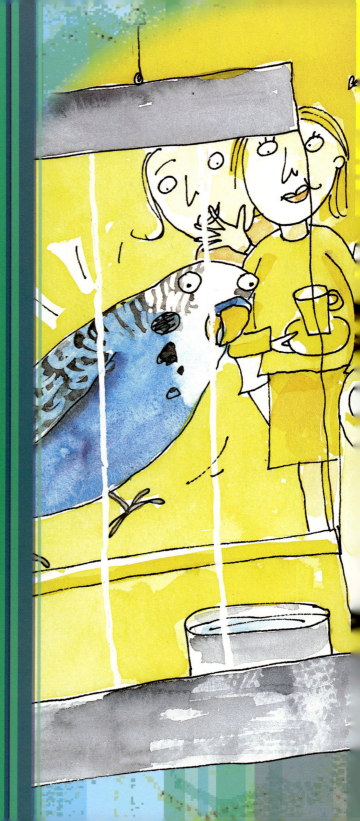

Sometimes, when there were strangers about, Peter got excited. He bobbed up and down and strutted around his cage, like a famous film star on a stage.

"Hello! Hello! Quark! Quark! Who's a pretty boy? Bedtime, Peter! Pop goes the weasel. Quark! Quark! Good morning, Grandma! Mary had a little lamb! Hello! Hello! Hello! Pop goes the weasel! Quark! Quark! Quark!"

Peter made Grandma happy. She treated him like a spoilt baby, always buying new toys for his cage or giving him new birdseed.

She talked to him continuously. "Who's a pretty boy? Who's a pretty boy?" she asked.

"Giz a bickie! Giz a bickie! Pop goes the weasel! Giz a bickie," he replied, bobbing up and down like a cheeky little boy.

Then one day Grandma got sick and had to go to hospital. She lay on the pillow – a plastic mask on her nose and her eyes closed. There were tubes in her arms and a big bag hanging behind her. When she breathed, it sounded like a fireman breathing through a rescue mask.

Every day on my way home from school, I visited Peter and fed him and let him out to stretch his wings. I told him that Grandma would be home soon. "She misses you!" I said. "She can't wait to see you again."

"Hello! Hello! Giz a bickie! Pop goes the weasel! Wake up, Grandma. Quark! Quark!" replied Peter.

Predict:

What do you think will happen in the story now?

Every night, Mum took me to see Grandma. She lay sleeping and her breath came out as a deep, husky, empty sound through her mask. "Peter says he loves you," I told Grandma. "He wants you to come home soon." She didn't answer . . . but I knew she could hear.

Mum and I visited Grandma every night for a long time. Every night I held Grandma's hand and listened to her loud breathing inside her mask. "Shhuuuushh! Shhhuuushh!" Every night I told Grandma, "Peter loves you, Grandma. He wants you to come home."

"She's not getting better," the doctor told Mum. "We can't do anything more."

Mum cried when she told Dad. "The doctors are doing all they can," she said. "There's nothing more we can do."

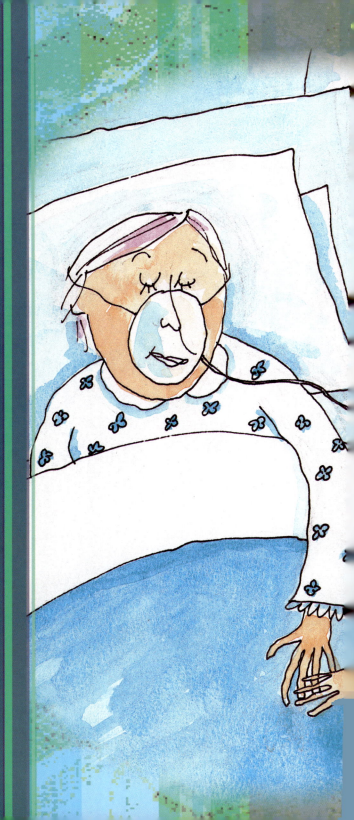

Clarify:

husky

A wheezy
B throaty/hoarse
C loud

A, B or C ?

That night in bed, I cried when I thought about Grandma. I knew there was something more I could do. I knew how to make her better. "Tomorrow, Grandma," I promised. "Tomorrow I will make you well."

Next morning I went to Grandma's house to feed Peter and let him out for a fly. "Hello, Peter," I said.

"Giz a bickie! Giz a bickie! Pop goes the weasel!" He was excited to see me. "Pop goes the weasel! Pop goes the weasel! Pop goes the weasel! Quark! Quark! Quark! Wake up, Grandma!"

I carried Peter to the hospital in his cage.

Question:

Why do you think the narrator took the budgie to the hospital?

I went up in the lift and walked along the corridor towards Grandma's room. "You talk to her, Peter. You tell her to get better."

"Pop goes the weasel!" sang Peter in his cheeky voice.

Then, just as I got to Grandma's door, a doctor stopped me. "Hey! Young man!" she said. "You can't take a budgie in there. That lady is sick. You will make her worse."

She took me by the arm and started to lead me away from Grandma's room. "No! No!" I cried. "Peter won't make Grandma sick. He's her best friend. He'll make her better."

"I'm sorry," said the doctor. "I can't let you take a budgie in there. It's against the rules."

Inference:

What can you infer about the character of the doctor from the following words? *"I can't let you take a budgie in there. It's against the rules."*

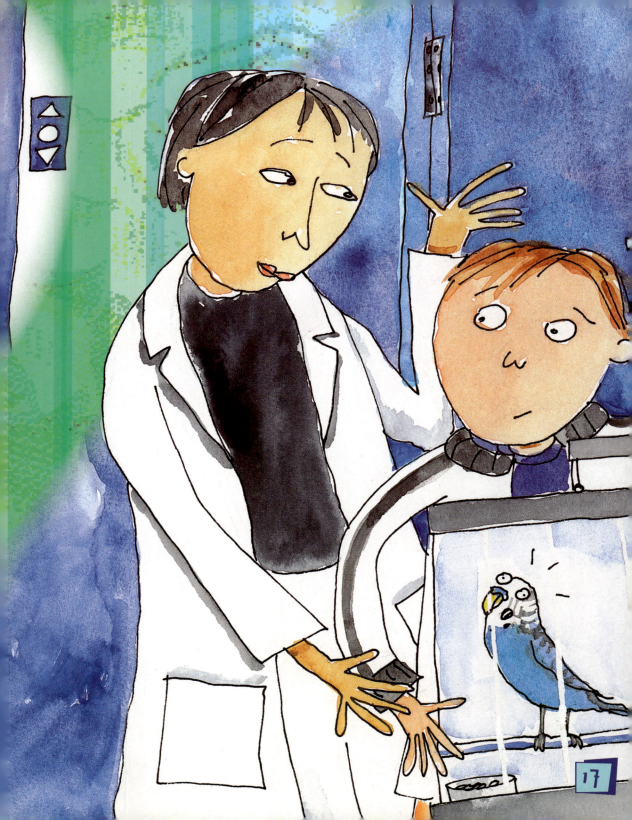

I wanted to cry. I tried to break away from the doctor and run back to Grandma's room but she wouldn't let me, so I sat down on the floor and cried anyway.

Peter thought I wanted to play and got excited. "Quark! Quark! Quark!" he squawked cheekily, bobbing up and down across his swing. "Wake up, Grandma! Wake up, Grandma! Giz a bickie! Quark! Quark! Wake up, Grandma! Wake up, Grandma! Wake up, Grandma!"

The doctor heard Peter showing off and started laughing. "I see what you mean," she said. "He must be a very good friend."

The doctor looked at me and Peter for a long time . . .

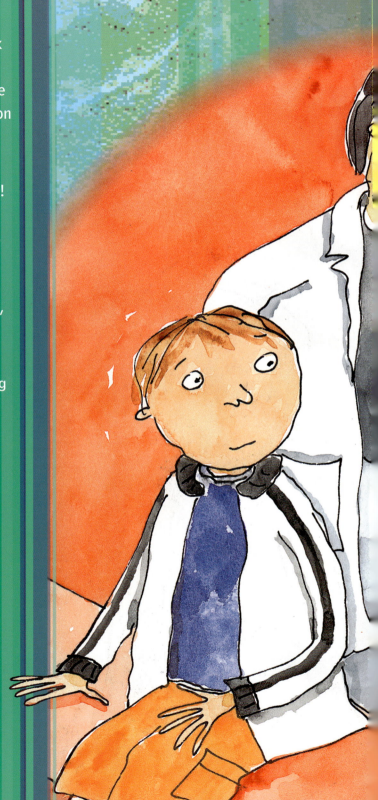

"Look," she said at last. "Maybe you are right. Maybe Peter's medicine can do what my doctor's medicine can't do."

I walked back along the corridor with the doctor to Grandma's room. I put Peter's cage on a table near the window, in the sun beside her bed.

For once Peter was quiet. He stood on his swing looking around the room. He had a drink of water. He pecked at his mirror. He jumped onto a perch and scratched the feathers under his eye.

"Come on, Peter," I said. "Say something!"

"Perhaps he is shy in front of strangers," said the doctor.

"No," I said. "He likes to show off. He's a proper skite!"

"Come on, Peter! Say something," I begged.

Peter started walking backwards and forwards along his perch. Faster and faster he strutted, his head bobbing up and down, up and down, up and down.

"Wake up, Grandma!" he screeched. "Wake up, Grandma! Wake up, Grandma! Quark! Quark! Giz a bickie! Pop goes the weasel! Wake up, Grandma! Wake up, Grandma! Quark! Quark! Quark!"

The doctor laughed. "I see what you mean," she said. "He really is a show-off."

"Wake up, Grandma! Wake up, Grandma! Wake up, Grandma!" Peter screeched.

But Grandma didn't move. She lay still on her pillow. "Shuuuuush! Shuuuuuush! Shuuuuush!" sounded her breath inside her mask.

"Wake up, Grandma! Wake up, Grandma!"

I watched Grandma, hoping for a miracle. But she didn't move. She didn't say anything. She just kept breathing loudly. "Keep talking, Peter! Don't stop!" I said.

"Shuuuuuush! Shuuuush!" breathed Grandma.

The doctor patted me on the head. "Don't expect too much," she said. "Your Grandma is very sick. Even Peter may not be able to make her well."

Wake up, Grandma!

Wake up, Grandma!

Wake up, Grandma!

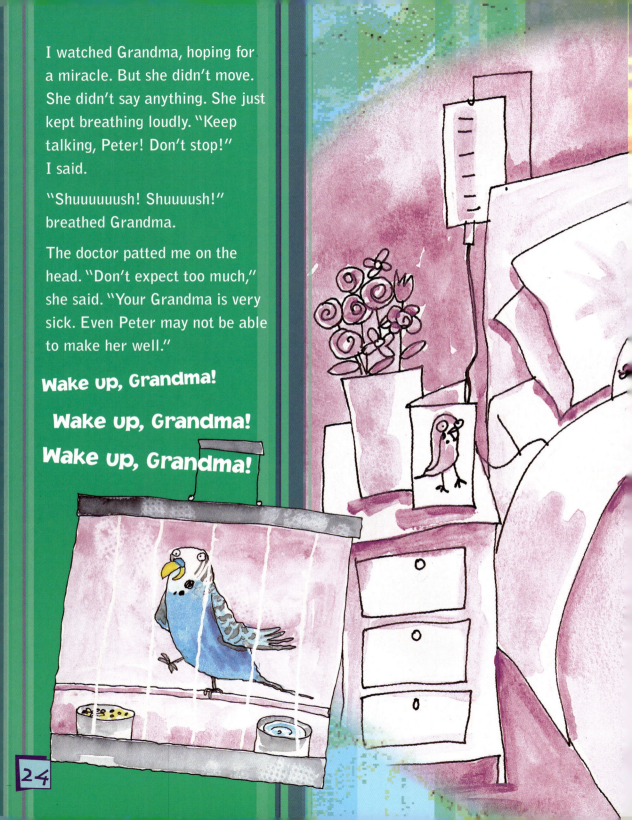

She just kept breathing loudly.

Emotions:

What words would you use to describe how the narrator is feeling now?

calm   frustrated   desperate   angry   unhappy   sad   anxious

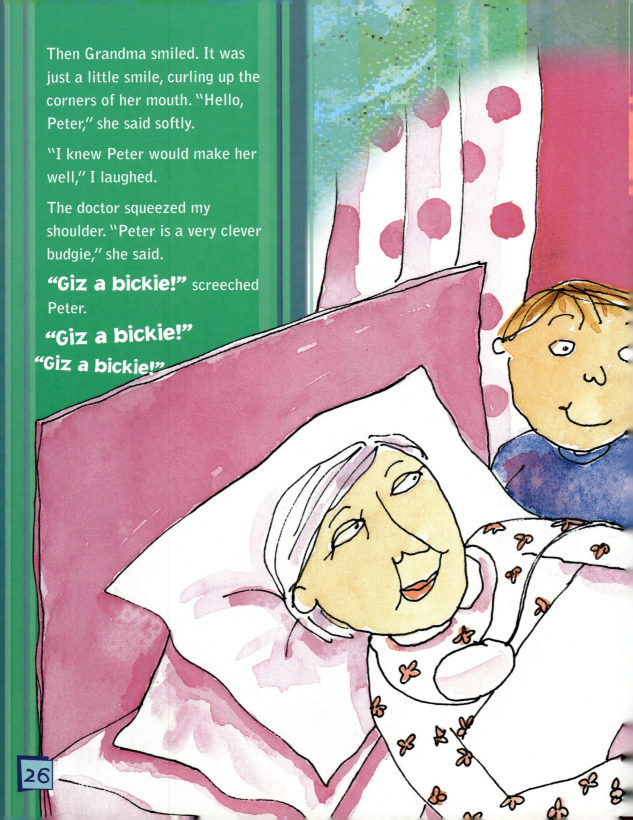

Then Grandma smiled. It was just a little smile, curling up the corners of her mouth. "Hello, Peter," she said softly.

"I knew Peter would make her well," I laughed.

The doctor squeezed my shoulder. "Peter is a very clever budgie," she said.

"Giz a bickie!" screeched Peter.

"Giz a bickie!"

"Giz a bickie!"

Summary:

What key points would you put in a summary of *Grandma's Budgie*?

- The narrator gave Grandma a budgie so she wouldn't be lonely.
- Grandma taught the budgie to talk.
- Grandma got sick and went to hospital.
- The doctor said Grandma wasn't getting better.
- The narrator took the budgie to visit Grandma in the hospital.
- The doctor said budgies were not allowed in the hospital.
- The narrator cried.
- The budgie made the doctor laugh and was allowed into the hospital.
- Grandma woke up and smiled at the budgie.

Think About the Text

Making connections – What connections can you make to the text?

- friendship
- loneliness
- anxiety
- sadness
- thoughtfulness
- kindness
- compassion

Text to Self

Text to Text

Talk about other stories you may have read that have similar features. Compare the stories.

Text to World

Talk about situations in the world that might connect to elements in the story.

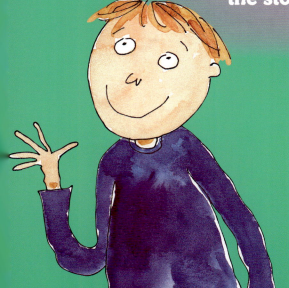

Planning a Personal Recount

1 Think about an introduction

Think about:

Who

When

... when I was a kid

Where

... at the hospital

What

2 Think about events in order of sequence

| The narrator gave Grandma a budgie so she wouldn't be lonely. | → | Grandma got sick and went to hospital. | → | The doctor said Grandma wasn't getting better. |

| The narrator took the budgie to visit Grandma in the hospital. | → | The doctor said budgies were not allowed in the hospital. | → | The budgie made the doctor laugh and was allowed into the hospital. |

3 Think about the conclusion

Grandma woke up and smiled at the budgie.

In a Personal Recount ...

A the narrator's own responses and reactions are recorded

B events are recorded in a sequence and links are made to do with time

C events all relate to one particular occasion, happening or idea

D there is a conclusion at the end, that could include an interpretation of events or a personal comment

E past tense is used

F first person is used

G the narrator was personally involved in the event